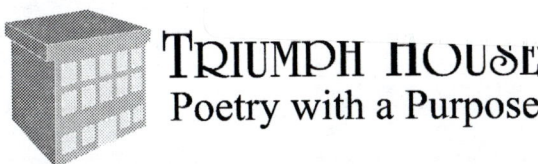

HANDS OF FAITH

Edited by

Steve Twelvetree

*To Gill & Eric
Lots of Love
Stella
xx*

First published in Great Britain in 2000 by
TRIUMPH HOUSE
Remus House,
Coltsfoot Drive,
Woodston,
Peterborough, PE2 9JX
Telephone (01733) 898102

All Rights Reserved

Copyright Contributors 1999

HB ISBN 1 86161 701 1
SB ISBN 1 86161 706 2

FOREWORD

Hands Of Faith is a collection of poetry written by poets from many different walks of life. The writers have come together to express the thoughts of Christians all over the world, but each gives their own personal perspective about faith, hope, belief and the many elements that make and mould our lives. Each poet has a story to tell, a message to share or a few words of comfort they want to pass on to others. With such a wide variety of views on the many things that we hold close to our hearts, this anthology is a must for anybody in need of Christian inspiration.

Steve Twelvetree
Editor

CONTENTS

Holding Others Up To Live	Edward Christian	1
Prayer For God's Guidance	M Birtles	2
Friends	A Tarbox	3
One Last Thing	Rev Colin Gordon-Farleigh	4
Wishing	Isabella Buchan	5
Jesus Is Lord	Derek G Bond	6
He Heals The Broken Heart	P Stratton	7
A Hymn	Margaret E Siddans	8
Rendezvous With God	Jamie Richards	9
Sunday Congregation	Sarah Girdlestone	10
The Greatest Of Great Men	Frances Shenton	11
Millennium	L Clark	12
No Other Way	Chris Saunders	13
The Whitsun Comforter	Martin Burr	14
Don't Fear The Night	Sheryl Williamson	15
Worship	John G Studley	16
Return To Horeb	G Jones	17
Freedom For All	M Lawson	18
The Donkey	B Boon	19
Precious Memories	F Sidaway	20
Journey's End	Julia Cutting	21
All Sunshine Makes A Desert	Karen Husband	22
Christmas	Audrey Coe	23
Mystical Egypt	Freda Bill	24
Snowflakes	Ann Marsh	25
Time	Stella Hughes	26
No Tears In Heaven	Anne M Smithers	27
Friends	Olive L Groom	28
What	Jane Wade	29
Communicate Love	June Goodair	30
Do You Remember	D Dinkel	31
Looking Back (14 Years On)	Eileen K Bunn	32
Mothers	Val Francis	33
The Warmth Of A Smile	Albert Gornley	34
Love's Gift	Mary Veronica Ciarella Murray	35
What Follows The Amen?	Margaret Cockbain	36

Respect	A Harrison	37
Beautiful Seasons	Joy Firth	38
Forget-Me-Nots	Barbara Hampson	39
Solace	Alfa	40
He Is Risen	Hazel Guest	42
Forgive Us Lord	Helen Lockwood	43
Other Love	Elizabeth Grant	44
It's All There	Richard Clewlow	45
A Morning Prayer	Kathleen Webb	46
The New Millennium	Dawn Rudderham-Thornhill	47
Divine Love	Jeannine Anderson Hall	48
Guiding Light	Chrystal Wanstall	49
Almighty Fear	Pettr Manson-Herrod	50
Fairground Meeting	Irene Grant	51
Open Thou Our Eyes	Andrew Duncan	52
The Road Home	Isobel Buchanan	53
Treasure Trove	Kathleen McQueen	54
A Walk By The Canal	R M Rawlings	55
His Promise	E Morgan	56
Gifts	D Irvine	57
The Convent	A Kendall	58
In Such A Night As This	Angela Matheson	59
The Trees	G Graham	60
To God	Liz Dicken	61
The Composer's Death	J H Higginson	62
What's A Poem?	Richard Stoker	63
To You Lord The Glory	Cecilia Skudder	64
Like A Child	Catherine Can	65
The Nurse Is	Eleanor Thomas	66
Untitled	Steve Storey	67
Those Books!	Lilian Loftus	68
Vandalism	Beryl Wagner	69
Morning	Clair Green	70
A Plea	Doris Riley	71
The Tree	M Hunter	72
Always! Remember!	E Coke	73
Ode To A Dead Dog	A E Fox	74
A Holiday In Wales	Nan Gosling	75

I Believe, I Believe, I Believe	Barbara Smith	76
The Truth Will Set You Free	Pauline Wilkins	77
Are You Willing?	S Sanders	78
The Holy Spirit	Anne Smith	79
Life's Passing	B Johnson	80
Friendship	Kathleen Jay	81
With God By Your Side	R Dilks	82
The Sorrowful Passion	John Atherton	83
A Day Amidst Nature	Deborah Thompson	84
We Cannot Know	Rita Hillier	85
Redeem	Joy Sheridan	86
Inspiration	Lucille Norton-Ercan	87
Pilgrim's Regress	Douglas Lawrie	88
Evening	Robert A Hardwidge	89
Prisoner's Prayer	Jamesie Gardner	90
I Pray	Margaret Rankin	91
Tinsel On The Xmas Tree	M Hudson	92
Confidence	Lily H O'Reilly	93
To The Uttermost Jesus Saves	Rose Culley	94
The Valley Of The Shadow	Anne Smith	95
The Preacher	Fred Hill	96
Live Within My Heart	Kevin P S Collins	97
Changing	Don Friar	98
Questions?	Avis Ciceri	99
One Sleepless Night	Gwen Tominey	100
Christ Child 2000	C Morris	101
Two Thousand Years	Ena Stanmore	102
Holiness Divine	Margaret Jackson	103
Worthy To Be Praised	Joan Marsh	104
Day Six	David Lord	105
Journey's End	Carolyn M Sill	106
To Mother - 1975	Celia Ann Islam	107
When Sunday Comes	M Milliken	108
Hand Power	Rita White	109
The Wisemen	Valerie Kirwood Edwards	110
He Knows The Cross We Have To Bear	Doreen Craig	111
In You We Trust	Hugh Campbell	112

Keep A Watch On Your Words	Frank Scott	113
Don't Worry Rap	Heather M Simpson	114
Spring's Awakening	Isobel Laffin	115
Approaching The Twenty-First Century	June Legg	116
The Gospel According To You	Robert Gerald	117
Joyous Times	Elizabeth M Dowler	118
Tears Of Peace	Bryon J Jones	119
Pope John Paul Paid A Visit	F N Fairchild	120
The Year Of Our Lord 2000	Marjorie Jones	121
The Christmas Season	Helen Manson	122
God's Love	Angela Kellie	123
Guardian Angel	Doris Rowe	124
To Eventide	R Large	125
The Millennium Message	Bessie Martin	126
My Belief	Trisha Moreton	127
A Summer Stroll	Helen Knott	128
Building	Elsie Birch	129
Heaven	Margaret Turner	130
To Live Forever	Sean Nixon-Smith	131
A Gift For Christmas	Barbara Ashworth	132
Tree Surgeon	Robert D Shooter	133
God's Millennium	Joy Francis	134
Goodbye Margaret, Goodbye Stuart	Tom Hicks	135
Sonnet To A Millennium Hope	Thomas H Woods	136
In Troubled Times	Ian Squire	137
The Word	Ivy Squires	138
Untitled	Ann Langley	139
A New Beginning	Olwen Counsell	140
Prayer For Radar	Linda Zulaica	141
I Wonder	Jean Logan	142

HOLDING OTHERS UP TO LIVE
O Lord, open Thou my lips; and my mouth shall show forth Thy praise
Psalm 51:15

Speak! My tongue for the Lord Jesus.
Write! My pen to His command.
See O eyes. Be ever watchful,
Helping others understand.
Hold me steadfast saviour Jesus.
Lead me to your side to live.
Keep me constant in your service
Holding others up to live.

Hold my hand O loving Father.
Lead me to your throne, above.
Pour through me Your Holy Spirit
Passing others up to love.
Guide my footsteps! Loving Saviour.
Lead me to Your pool, to give
Living water, in full measure
Holding others up to live.

Edward Christian

PRAYER FOR GOD'S GUIDANCE

Oh Lord our Gracious Father
Look down on me today,
Give me the will to conquer
The sins that come my way.

Oh Lord give me a vision
That I may see the sight
Of Guardian Angels watching
In the stillness of the night.

Oh Lord give me a hearing
That I may hear the call
Of trumpets sounding loudly
By Thy celestial wall.

Oh Lord give me a foothold
That I may place my feet
Along the heavenly pathway
Where Thine Apostles meet.

Oh Lord give me a feeling
That Thou art always near
When I despair or falter
Have nothing for to fear.

Oh Lord give me a heart
That I may turn to thee
And ask for Thy forgiveness
When evil I may be.

Oh Lord give me a sense of gratitude
A chance to say 'Thank you'
For all the gifts bestowed on me
And the things I love to do.

M Birtles

FRIENDS

Everybody needs a friend
To help them on their way,
With maybe just a phone call
To check that they're OK.
A simple word of greeting
To a stranger passing by,
A nod, a smile, a cheerful wave
Can lift their spirits high.
If you're feeling rather lonesome,
Or someone's let you down
Remember that a happy face
looks better than a frown.
You won't encourage others
If you look forever blue,
So always try to wear a smile,
It's a simple thing to do.
When you wake up in the morning
Make a promise that today,
You're going to help somebody
And guide them on their way.
If you keep that smile upon your face
In almost everything you do,
You'll find that all the folk you meet
Will feel much brighter too.

A Tarbox

ONE LAST THING

Oh Lord, if I should stumble
As I journey on life's way;
If I should wander from the path
You've planned for me this day;
If I should find that I am left
Within this world of care,
Just one last thing to pray for,
Let it be that You are there.

Let me reach out to touch You,
To place my hand in Thine:
Then turn my feet to tread once more
Upon Your path divine.
If I should feel that I am left
With this one thought to share,
Let me praise You for the love
That answers every prayer.

Rev Colin Gordon-Farleigh

WISHING

Wishing, wishing, wishing,
Won't get you very far;
Though it's wishing for a fortune,
Or wishing on a star;
Instead of only wishing
Come on, and say I can;
And try to make a better life
And be a better man;
Thank God for all your blessings
Though large, or very small;
Remember he is watching
For He is God of all;
You only have to ask Him
And He will enter in;
And fill your heart with gladness
And take away your sin;
You won't need any wishing
For you've got all you need
When you take God into your heart
Well, you are rich indeed.

Isabella Buchan

JESUS IS LORD

Jesus is Lord,
Jesus is king,
With Him as a pal,
I can do anything.

Jesus is good,
Jesus is right,
Come out you evil ones,
We'll give you a fight.

Jesus is the one
And God's only son,
Being a Christian
Can be so much fun.

Jesus the leader,
Jesus the guide,
He is always with you,
Always by your side.

Jesus our teacher,
Listen to the word,
That's the best news
I have ever heard.

Jesus our head,
Jesus is love,
He'll meet us again,
Up in heaven above.

__Derek G Bond__

HE HEALS THE BROKEN HEART

The mighty God of whose command
Creation had its part,
Who names and counts the number of the stars
Heals the broken heart.
The distance between those myriad orbs
And breaking heart of man
Seems vast, immeasurable - a gulf
The human thought can span.

But God in human flesh disguised
In person of His Son,
Rejected, sorrowful, despised
The perfect, sinless one
Stooping beneath the heavy cross
With bleeding, thorn-crowned head,
Amid the jeering, hateful, throng
To Calvary was led.

Dying there between Earth and heaven
Atoning for man's sin,
The Son of man - yet Son of God
Did bridge that gulf between
Those glistening gems and hearts that break
The stars and human tears,
Thus contemplating love divine
                all doubting disappears.

Each throb in grief-torn human heart
Is echoed in His own,
The secret tear, though shed apart
Is never shed alone.
O condescending, matchless love,
O gracious majesty
That He who spins the world in space
Reveals such sympathy.

P Stratton

A Hymn
Based On Habakkuk 3: 17-19 and 2:4

Although the fig tree bears no fruit,
The vine and olive do not yield,
No profit comes from sheep or beasts,
No produce from the harvest field,

My Saviour God is all my joy;
In Him alone I will rejoice.
He is the constant, sovereign Lord;
To Him I lift my heart and voice.

Just as the strong, sure-footed deer
Leap up the hills from height to height,
So God the Lord, my strength, my stay,
Makes me triumph in His might.

My confidence is in my God.
'By faith the just shall live,' I read.
This faith He gives me through His Son,
Who is my Lord and God indeed.

Margaret E Siddans

RENDEZVOUS WITH GOD

Headlights flash, a car horn blares,
Within my mind a firework flares.
My life flashes past before my eyes
And then I'm soaring through the skies.
I've left this world a lowly baker
On my way to meet my maker.
Once in heaven God explains
'Your time has not yet come young Baines,
But before you go back down below
A gift on you I shall bestow.'

'Come closer child,' the great man whispers,
whilst in his eyes divine light glisters.
'What I reveal now is sacred to life,
You must never divulge it to children nor wife.
For if you were foolish enough, say, to tell,
Such a crime would be punishable by . . . eternal hell!
So listen quite carefully, I shall say this just once.
The meaning of life is . . .'

'Stand clear!' cried the doctor, 'he's coming round now.
Everyone, nurses, you may all take a bow
For despite all the shouting and sweat and the weariness
We have saved this poor man from a near-death experience.'
Later, recovering alone and unfed
A woman and two children show up next to my bed.
Their faces all seem to be vaguely familiar,
Though I reason it's just that my own is quite similar.
What had just happened, where had I been?
Had someone just spoken to me during a dream?
'Hello, my darling, we've brought you some freesias.
We're sorry to hear about your permanent amnesia.'

Jamie Richards (18)

SUNDAY CONGREGATION

Quick feet, late feet, holy slowly feet.
Same seat every week.
Hands loose, hands clasped, holding children, holding hope.

All eyes look ahead, all ears catch the sounds,
But the minds, they are individual.
They think of friends, those dead,
They spring from the child misbehaving, to the lunch,
                          to where shall we go tomorrow?

Some are full of fear, that's why they are here.
If only I keep coming it will be all right.
All different thoughts, but all the same.

Like every couple who stand ready to marry,
Whatever happens once they leave,
For those few moments they mean it,
It is real.

Sarah Girdlestone

THE GREATEST OF GREAT MEN

After reading of the world's great men
Over their deeds I did pour.
A vision came to me then
And this is what I saw.

I saw thousands of poppies blowing in the wind,
The poppies though faceless all had wings.
Such an aura of sadness met my eyes
As they gazed upwards to the skies.

Johnny laying down his coat to enfold
Tommy, wounded and dying, he was cold.
Joe, running around, his reason and sight gone,
The never to be forgotten, The Battle of the Somme.

The vision fades, they are poppies once again
Stretching out to vale and glen.
I humbly salute you
The greatest of great men.

Frances Shenton

MILLENNIUM

M any preparations have been made for this new year,
I   t's a time for families and friends to share with cheer,
L oving couples are choosing this day to give a 'ring',
L ots of fireworks and parties will be happening,
E xciting feelings grow as celebrations near a start,
N ow, soon, church bells' welcome chimes will gladden every heart,
N ew beginnings, new plans and new hopes for future peace,
I   n all people the prayer is for war and pain to cease.
U nited for this unique experience round the world to come,
M ake the most of the moments of this millennium.

L Clark

No Other Way

Have you ever stopped to think
What God has done for you?
How his love and peace can give you strength
Whate'er you have to do.

How the gifts of his creation
Surround us every day.
But so often we ignore them,
More concerned with our own way.

How he sent his Son to live on earth,
In human form he came.
A lowly stable saw his birth,
Jesus was his name.

For him there was no princely home,
A carpenter was his trade.
But sure of his Father's constant love
He trusted and obeyed.

How Jesus taught of that great love,
To help to make us see
That by his death and resurrection
He was saving you and me.

How everlasting life we have
By his death upon the cross.
Such wondrous love so freely given,
Unbelief is certain loss.

So let God rule within your heart
Through each and every day.
Trust in him to lead and guide
There is no other way.

Chris Saunders

THE WHITSUN COMFORTER

For night upon two thousand years,
Hath earth been pleased to know
That from the highest heav'n appears
The Whitsun Comfort flow.

When life becomes a storm-tossed barque,
Above the clouds a glow
Pours out a light to light the dark,
The Whitsun Comfort flow.

When pain and sorrow rend ou rhearts,
Upon this earth below,
Lift up your hearts; thank God who starts
The Whitsun Comfort flow.

When all the world against us seems
And we are feeling low,
Let us look up to heav'n whence teams
The Whitsun Comfort flow.

There is a little voice so deep
Within our hearts we know,
Which bids us aye in contact keep
With Whitsun Comfort's flow.

For nigh upon two thousand years
This comfort hath been so:
Two thousand more, dry thou their tears,
O Whitsun Comfort's flow.

Martin Burr

DON'T FEAR THE NIGHT

I saw him steal along the ground;
He was silent, never making a sound
Suddenly he reached me, and then
Having overshadowed me, was gone again
By the lit doorway in the hall.

I saw him creeping along the wall
His shadow created darkness everywhere
His presence simply filled the air,
I felt tiny like a little kid:
I almost ran, I nearly hid
But I decided instead to brave it out,
He was only *Night*, I could last him out.

So I faced the Night, and he
Said: 'It's time to sleep, hush - don't fear me . . .'

Sheryl Williamson

WORSHIP

The past is history, now the future's in view,
God is in control, that gives comfort too.
Writing thus we ponder, the wonder of that love,
Which drew salvation's plan, in a glory land above.

While we think of our Lord, the fact of His deity,
In numerous acts, performed with such piety,
Truly God's glory is expressed in that face,
Extolling a person with unusual grace.

But man, oh so wicked, disfigured it so,
Buffeting, tugging, where hair used to grow,
That features, we read, were hard to define,
Of that suffering man, our Saviour divine.

They crowned Him too, with a crown of thorn
And smote it hard, with such vicious scorn,
then bearing the cross, to Calvary He went
To pour out His blood, till all life was spent.

Redemption's plan required a victim so pure,
That only our Lord Himself could endure -
God's wrath upon sin, when darkness prevailed,
For Jesus alone knew what it entailed.

Our crucified Lord who rose from the dead,
Is seated in heaven with glory crowned head,
We bow then in worship, and worship always,
For obtaining salvation, the dark Calvary way.

Though dark was the Cross, the glory shines through,
For Jesus our saviour left nothing to do,
We are redeemed, through God's only Son,
For the work of redemption forever is done.

Hallelujah, hallelujah, hallelujah for the cross.

John G Studley

RETURN TO HOREB

Let the waters divide:-
The enemy drown,
Stand in the mist on the mountain
Hidden from the footprints of progress
Beneath the deepening sands of years
The answers lie buried, silent,
Though born with the sound of thunder.
The questions remain.

Let the nations divide:
The world drown.
Emerge through the rising mists of shame
Hung darkly over hidden ways,
Ignored through fear, born of ignorance,
The promise remains.

Let East and West divide:-
Detente is dead.
Lie in the dust of distrust
In a desert it began
In a desert we remain,
Exposed to the sun,
Bleached clean at journey's end.
Nothing remains.

Let the clouds divide:-
The mountains survive.
Follow the path trod by the prophet
Listen for the voice still echoing down
The years: return to Horeb
And having heard, take heed
And hope remains.

G Jones

FREEDOM FOR ALL

God bless those who have no freedom
Throughout this world of ours
Where rights are taken from them
By wrongful governing powers,
Comfort them in their anguish
And grant O Lord that we
May help to put asunder
And set the people free.

God bless the little children
Who cannot understand
Why they should be divided
In their God-given land.
The hungry and the homeless
Embrace them with your love
And through the grace of Jesus
Their sufferings overcome.

The Bible plainly tells us
That we are one in Christ
There should be no race distinction
If skin be black or white.
We pray that through your blessing
That soon will come the day
When hearts of men will change
And follow in Christ's way.

M Lawson

THE DONKEY

Some call me just a common ass
And mock my hideous bray,
But I possess a secret
And care not what they say.
Of all the beasts I am so proud,
As I recall that day,
I trotted through a noisy crowd
Who threw palms in my way.
Upon my back I carried a man,
Messiah was his name,
His hands so gentle held my head
To calm me through the din.
My fearfulness of crowds soon fled
With confidence from Him.
Although some passed me by with scorn
And beat and nagged me on
Mine is the joy for I was born
To carry Christ, God's son.

B Boon

Precious Memories

A new year dawns as the old year goes,
Embracing all our joys and woes,
Life is full of ups and downs,
Joys and tears, laughter and frowns,
Over life's horizon they disappear,
Friends and relatives of yesteryear,
Elongated shadows strew our path,
Echoing voices we used to hear laugh,
Indelibly printed on human minds
Are living pictures of various kinds,
Precious memories, not skeletons in cupboards,
Or selfish thoughts like a miser hoards,
Like old buildings crumbling in dust
Or like cheap trinkets turned to rust.
They are treasured values of bygone years,
Warmly sealed by love, laughter and tears,
For memory is a precious gift from God above,
An everlasting sign of His great love
To help us remember everything good.

F Sidaway

JOURNEY'S END

New to the fold
We set out on level path
Wrapped in comfortable clothing,
Feet snug as we stride,
Smiling confidently,
Into an undisclosed future:
Knowing journey's end.

Cruel sharp stones begin
To pierce footwear.
Cold biting winds
Penetrate thick woollens.
But confidence, focusing
On ultimate destination,
Weathers the elements.

Road littered with jagged rocks
Inclines steeply.
Rain lashes wind-chapped face.
Saturated woollens weighing heavily
Confidence loses buoyancy.
Terrain testing endurance,
Commitment to one's path.

Then into vision steps
A welcome friend
Offering a warm haven,
Refreshing companionship.
Kitted out in all-weather 'armour',
Bold strides continue with reinforced
Confidence towards journey's end.

Julia Cutting

ALL SUNSHINE MAKES A DESERT

'All sunshine makes a desert.'
No truer words were said,
That through life's times of sunshine
Some teardrops must be shed.

Let's take as an example,
The newly planted seeds,
Of course they need the sunshine
But that's not all to fill their needs.

The gentle fall of raindrops
Will quench the seedlings thirst
And help it to grow stronger
'til it's final glory bursts.

Our life and soul compare to this,
We need that rainfall too
To wash away the old things
And prepare us for the new.

Without the tears and sunshine
Life would be rather bland,
There'd be no green, no colour,
Just hot and dusty land.

So, when rain clouds are forming
And the tears begin to flow,
Don't lose heart, it has to be
It gives us a chance to grow.

Karen Husband

CHRISTMAS

Let's forget about the presents,
Let's forget about the lights,
Let's forget about the Christmas trees,
Let's forget those party nights.
Let's put Christ back into Christmas
And remember why he came
To save a world in darkness,
A people lost in shame.
Born a babe in Bethlehem
He grew to be a man
Who loved and healed and saved the lost,
As was his Father's plan.
So let's hail our precious Saviour
Alive in us today
And thank him on his birthday
For coming here to stay.

Audrey Coe

MYSTICAL EGYPT

The colour of the sun is red, a'glowing in the night,
The palms sway to and fro, with rhythm capturing the light.
You look across the river to the mountains so forlorn,
The sun goes to the underworld and in the morning is reborn.
The temples tall and mystical, reaching to the sky.
Why did they let them to ruin, all I can do is sigh.
The king and queens were buried in the mountains for a tomb,
They said they'd be reborn again by Isis in her womb.
The treasures that were buried in that dark, forgotten place,
Only one was found intact, when Howard Carter saw his face.
He's been there just awaiting for 3,000 years or more.
The grave-robbers had been in there, things strewn across the floor.
A light was struck, no poison gas, the people gave a sigh,
They hadn't searched the valley for years, to give up now and die.
The glint of gold was everywhere to everyone's delight,
Was there a curse upon this tomb, the believers they took flight.
Howard Carter took ten years or more to catalogue his find,
I don't think Tutankhamun, after all those years, did mind,
He's gone down now in history, his mummy's been returned,
Oh so glad I visited mystical Egypt, again I will return.

Freda Bill

SNOWFLAKES

They fall to earth and kiss the ground
Each one unlike its neighbour
But together they have strength
Now let me beg a favour.

As on your way you travel,
With heavy heart perhaps.
Remember friends, like snowflakes
Can lift you when you lapse.

For there is strength in unity,
It does not think of pride
It only looks to love and care,
It does not cast aside.

Keep contact then with those who care
And those who do and those who dare
Keep in your heart those cherished dreams
Life will not burst out at the seams.

Go on dreaming,
Learn to achieve
What is right
Go on believe.

Believe in love and care and trust
And in yourself, that is a must,
Believe in truth and unity,
Believe for you and not for me.

Ann Marsh

TIME

Lord I am here and I live for today, not tomorrow,
I live for what today can bring,
Not for what I can take out of it,
But what I can give to it.
I can approach it with fear or with joy and expectation
And my love of my Lord.
I can be low of spirit, or full of hope.
Tomorrow never comes for it is today,
Today has turned into yesterday.
Live for each moment and give thanks unto the Lord
For time runs through your fingers
Like grains of sand.

Stella Hughes

NO TEARS IN HEAVEN

Though familiar pain of hunger
Be my daily wakening.
If famine is my here and now,
Tomorrow, meagre as today - but
I shall feast in heaven.

Though sacrifice is forced upon me
By the ravages of war.
Tears a precious loss of moisture
Thirst can ill afford to waste - but
I shall drink in heaven.

Children's fearful cries of terror
Wrench my heart that cannot help.
Fathers dead and mothers missing.
Babies, such as mine, are gone - but
We'll unite in heaven.

Anne M Smithers

FRIENDS

Do we choose them?
Do they choose us?
We seem to gain them without much fuss.
They warm our hearts,
Gladden our minds
And are among life's worthier finds.

Lonely the way,
Daunting and rough.
Even for loving families it's tough.
Families fade,
Lovers depart,
Who then is to mend the broken heart?

How odd it is
That on our way
We ignore One who would be our stay,
The unseen Friend,
Stalwart and strong,
Who waits at the door whatever goes wrong.

When all else fails,
He alone stands,
The Almighty Friend with uplifting hands.

Olive L Groom

WHAT

What can I do, is that what you say,
when you watch all the news on the TV each day.
What can I do about the poor and oppressed,
do you come away feeling thoroughly depressed?

Well, all is not lost, we can play our part,
the trouble is, just where do we start?
We start where we are, by being concerned,
just the sheer fact that our heads have been turned.

Then we look for some way to help where we can,
use our time wisely, help that poor man;
pray for God's world, feel compassion and care,
give what we can and learn how to share.

So don't feel downhearted by all that you see,
just look to your Lord and ask that you'll be,
used for his purpose today and tomorrow,
knowing you've eased just some of life's sorrow.

Jane Wade

COMMUNICATE LOVE

Father, Father, why is my tongue so still?
Why can't I exercise your will?
Why can I not reply to them?
Dear Lord, let me do this with my pen
Dear Lord, please let me communicate
That love is far better than hate.

This is the first commandment you said
I know it is true, because I read,
I read it when so young I was
This you said to do; because
To do His will and His command
Will give to us that just reward.

Thank you Lord for answering my prayer
peeling off fears layer by layer
To speak your word through my tongue
as I could, when I was young.
It was easier then, no fears I had,
but now at times I feel so sad,
it does not come easy to do your will,
much easier now when I am still.
Still, to hear your dear voice,
I wouldn't want any other choice
So thank you Lord, for all you do
allowing me; to communicate through you.

June Goodair

DO YOU REMEMBER

Do you remember
When I took you by the hand
And offered to take you
To the promised land.

Do you remember
Your apprehension, your fear
Yet still you travelled onwards
Your trust I held dear.

Your journey was difficult
The pathway was long
But my people walked together
And kept each other strong.

Do you remember
Do you see life's still the same
So much sin and suffering
Still no one to blame.

Please do remember
The strife we've lived through
With the strength we build together
There's a promised land in you.

D Dinkel

Looking Back (14 Years On)

I suffered with depression,
Clinical and real,
I thought my life had ended
With no more joy or zeal.

But then . . . You heard me crying
When I knelt down in prayer.
You said, 'Come here, my precious child,
For you I really care.'

You told me that you'd heal me -
You waved a magic wand;
You touched me - and you whispered,
'Your pain is now all gone.'

I suddenly felt different,
I knew my life had changed.
My burden had been lifted:
God had it all arranged.

I stood and looked around me
But couldn't see your face.
I heard your voice so softly say,
'My child, don't be afraid.'

Your touch was oh so gentle,
Your healing so complete.
I never will forget the day
The Lord and I would meet.

I cannot just say, 'Thank you'
It doesn't seem enough.
My King, My Lord, My Jesus,
My Healer, with a touch.

Eileen K Bunn

MOTHERS

What is a Mother? Where does one start?
For hers is the voice you hear with your heart.
Hers is the hand that mops away tears,
Chases the gremlins and banishes fear.

Hers is the presence that's constant and true,
Caring and loving, non-judgmental too.
Hers is the smile that brightens the day
The face that you see even when you're away.

Mothers are precious, their talents uncounted.
There isn't a problem they haven't surmounted.
Defender and champion, she'd fight to the death
In defence of her children, while she can draw breath.

God gave us Mothers to keep us from breaking
In the stresses and strains in this journey we're making.
So treat her respectfully. She is your mentor.
In the circle of life she is there at the centre.

Val Francis

THE WARMTH OF A SMILE

Time is of the essence
Time it cannot stand still
Time is what we make of it
Whether it be for good or ill
Time is something precious
Something we are searching for
How time irrevocably marches on
It's time for me to be up and gone
To pick up my bag, go out on the street
Hoping some friendly face I'll meet
Someone with whom I can linger a while
Exchanging a joke, a laugh and a smile
Then, bidding 'Adieu' going on my way
Happy with the start to my new born day
So tarry awhile as you're passing by
Tell them a story, bring a twinkle to their eye
Help them along, by word and song
Lighten their burden, with a smile
So smile each day as you go on your way
Each one smiling back will brighten your day.

Albert Gornley

LOVE'S GIFT

Love is the touch of a hand, a brush of the cheek
Meeting of souls making oneness complete
The growing together of two bashful hearts
Understanding forgiveness when things fall apart
Mother's love for her child that beams in her smile.

Tearful nights and fearful days
Till each has grown and found their way
The heartache that lies behind her smile
When each strays from the nest
Hoping for each the world at its best.

True happiness and joy she prays they all will be blessed
Love is a blanket that spreads all around
Creeps into the heart where sorrow is bound
It's the holding on and letting go
Of those you have loved and are no more
Love is the ovalness in life that binds this sad old world together
It rules supreme upon this earth though God alone
And will by God's good grace remain forever.

Mary Veronica Ciarella Murray

WHAT FOLLOWS THE AMEN?

And all the people said 'Amen'
And then set off for home.
To forget until this time next week -
Their God upon His throne.

And all the people said 'goodbye'
To friends, outside the door.
'That's twice today, I've been to church
Even God can't ask for more.'

And all the people hurried home -
To fireside and TV.
Not noticing that still, small voice,
'Slow down, remember me.'

When all the people said 'Amen'
After prayers and hymns and psalms.
They rushed away and left their God -
Ignored His outstretched arms.

Please don't do that. He's waiting still
To walk back home with you.
Open up your heart, your home, your life -
Let Him come and live there too.

Margaret Cockbain

RESPECT

I saw an old lady knelt by the side of a grave.
The weather was inclement. She was more than brave
Was she reaching for a husband, a boy or a girl?
Her thoughts I hope in a happy whirl.

Her pilgrimage from home to show love and respect,
To a bygone soul she will always recollect.
It's sad to think she would like to be hugged,
But as things are, maybe burglars or mugged.

I offered my hand, to help her to stand,
I had all the time in the world, nothing planned.
To offer her safety and help on her way
To give her love and respect makes it a perfect day.

A Harrison

BEAUTIFUL SEASONS

Spring, beautiful spring, heart warming,
With carefree breezes
And gentle rain upon face and earth.

Followed by summer and warmer days,
When buds have bloomed into rainbow colours
And the hues reflect in the rays of the sun.

Coming autumn delights the senses,
Leaves, majestic in their varied tints,
Fly with the wind before carpeting the ground.

And what of winter? With billowing clouds,
Boisterous winds, with rain and snow,
Preparing for rebirth and the coming of spring.

Joy Firth

FORGET-ME-NOTS

Forget-me-nots grew everywhere
In that month of May
Forget-me-nots, forget-me-nots
When Peter passed away
The garden it was covered
In this lovely sea of blue
No matter where she looked
There were forget-me-nots in view
Azaleas and rhodo's and ceonothus too
Surrounded by this carpet
Of a deep intensive blue
Her darling man departed
Had left her broken hearted
So happy had their life together been
A man so good and splendid
Until his life was ended
Oh what a lucky woman she had been
He'll always be remembered
She never will forget
But how she longed to have him by her side
Forget-me-nots still blooming
Whichever way she turned
Forget-me-nots still blooming far and wide.

Barbara Hampson

SOLACE

only a soft sound
of oars
.caresses
the silent water

in the boat
a lonely visitor
yearns
towards the island

hovering grey
greets the intruder's
despair
at dusk

glistening drops
escape
from careless leaves
drowning lilies

pushing aside
low, defenceless branches
he stumbles
over exposed willow roots

his face
is cold
and numb
from the evening mist

he follows
the narrow path
to the centre
of his longing

shivering in the breeze
thistles and nettles
no longer defend
their territory

lost, silver streaks
dart through
tired trees
before darkness wins

but when he touches
her grave
the stone warms
to his hand.

Alfa

HE IS RISEN

I have wonderful news to tell all who will listen
Our Lord died on the cross, but exclaimed I will come again
He is risen and among us now, He did not die in vain.
His promise was forgiveness for us all.

We are not worthy of such divine love
Which was given freely for all who believe
I feel His presence, I hear his words
I see the love in His eyes, for each and every one of us.

So long ago they put Him on a cross
He suffered humiliation, was falsely accused
Beaten cruelly and was scorned, my heart aches for Him
But He bore it all because He loved us.

The crown of thorns, the journey to Calvary
Carrying the dreadful cross, the nails they drove
Into His hands and feet, praise our wonderful saviour
He bore it all so our sins could be forgiven.

God sent his beloved son to die for us
Jesus obeyed the command of our heavenly father
We were made whole again, our duty is to obey
Just as Jesus did many years ago.

Because He is risen, He reigns in majesty, Praise God,
He is risen, He is risen, He is risen. Hallelujah.

Hazel Guest

FORGIVE US LORD

Forgive us Lord for the things we've done
to a world once lovely
and to your dear son.
We've poised your rivers.
Your lakes and your trees.
We've spoilt many woodlands,
Your beaches and seas.

We crucified Jesus
nailed Him to a tree.
He died on a cross
for sinners like me.
He came down to earth
from heaven above.
To teach us your ways
and show us your love.

We must have been blind Lord
for we failed to see
that this was our Saviour
hung there on the tree.

Forgive us dear Father
for our sinful ways
and help us to praise
you Lord
now and always.

Helen Lockwood

OTHER LOVE

I'm glad you love another
much more than you love me.
Because the other love you have
also loves me.

And as we give our heart to Him
this we do each day
it's plain to see, how blessed
we are in each and every way.

Being in love with Jesus
you will hear us say
having such love for Jesus
makes us love each other
more each passing day.

Elizabeth Grant

IT'S ALL THERE

Living only for now
This moment is precious
It means so much
We are still here
We mean to go
On to other things
Yes living for now
Living for the moment
Yes that is it
The truth best spoken
Otherwise it's all there.
Like it's all hid
Like it was before
Before all that happened
Life's journey is an
Hard one but we
All simply live it
That we do constantly
Live it often daily
It's a hard life
But you live it
An easy one is
Out of arms reach
So we are here
Still here yet again
What can you say
But holler your rottenness
Go up and die.

Richard Clewlow

A Morning Prayer

When you wake in the morning
kneel down and pray.
Giving thanks for your life
at the start of a new day.
For there's no truer friend than
the Lord up above
who was born in a stable and
died for the people He loved.
Put your faith, trust and life
in His hands every hour of the day.
Then He will guide you safely
along, the most difficult pathway
giving you hope, strength and
courage in whatever you do
until your life on earth is ended
and heavenly gates are opened
for you.

Kathleen Webb

THE NEW MILLENNIUM

The new millennium
Will come,
Make a date
For no hate.

And mark it with true love
That has come from above.

Those that are young
Have a new song to be sung.
Those that are old
Have a story to be told.

Those in the middle of life
Act now - and get rid of this strife!

Be a good friend
It's a start - not the end.
Act for peace
A blessed release.

Work for good
Don't shed blood!
Change the world
God - unfurled.

You are alive so act now - don't be dumb,
Don't wait for another millennium!

Dawn Rudderham-Thornhill

DIVINE LOVE

Upon the saving cross I see Him
In his awful agony,
And in His eyes is that reproach?
No! They are full of love for me.
Oh! How can I repay such love,
No sacrifice is asked nor deed
And yet there is a gift though small,
I can give my heart, my all.
For as He gave His life for me,
I will live my life,
For Him!

Jeannine Anderson Hall

GUIDING LIGHT

I am falling,
But I am solid on the ground.

I am flying
But I am locked in a cage.

My mind has a desire to learn,
But absorbs nothing.

I am laughing
But I am filled with grief.

I am lost,
But my world has not changed.

I am blind,
But I follow the guiding light.

Chrystal Wanstall

ALMIGHTY FEAR

I went to the edge of the world
And God was there.
I brushed past constantly
And hatred clutched my bones
And life swirled round, returning,
Fed into ever hungry maw
And fear was gripping there.

Time consumed my passion,
Derision formed. I wept.
Horizons came and went
And I was torn. Raw agony.
Almighty fear remains.

Pettr Manson-Herrod

FAIRGROUND MEETING

'Ye must be born again'
He kept repeating
He meant well
It is important
The two men
Got quite heated
In the discussion
As I tried to distance
Myself from the line of fire.
It was difficult to get a word in
The humble man produced a new testament
And then I understood how it had been
With the fisherman disciples.
Yet God could use the halting speech
An impediment - as I listen.
The voice is harsh and grating
Yet God can impress
That conversation could lead
To conversion, of the converted!
I do believe!

Irene Grant

OPEN THOU OUR EYES

The meenister has dune his darg;
he's facin nou retirement -
'A'm tired,' he says, 'and burned richt oot.'
'*His* peace is my requirement!'
He's nae that auld as auld age goes,
thur monie that much aulder
but nou he says he's lost the place
an finds the wind blaws caulder.
He doesna like the prospect nou,
that he'll be on his lane;
for aa the help he's had through life
nae much will nou remain.
T'is funny hoo, t'were ithers thus
he'd be aboot tae help them
but nou he's on his knees himsel
he's shair there's nane tae lift him.
'O ye o little faith' Christ said
then answered them their query,
'hae ye forgotten quite sae sune?
My love is for the weary
an if my love for you is there,
whate'er hae ye tae fear?
Ging on aboot yeir normal ways
an ken the Lord's aye near!

Andrew Duncan

THE ROAD HOME

As a soldier lay wounded on the battlefield,
He heard a voice, that gave him will.
He starts to pray,
Oh Lord, please help me make it home.
Or on this field, my spirit will roam,
The voice said 'Rise, you must go on
And when you're ready, I'll take you home'
The soldier got on to his feet,
He cried in pain,
Yet, his strength, He did again,
He'd just got to another field
And there to greet him, were his friends,
There was laughter and tears
And the soldier said to his friends,
'We have lots of years and when I
Get home, I'll go to church and pray,'
His words were true.
The soldier is in church each day
He is now a priest,
God took him home.

Isobel Buchanan

TREASURE TROVE

From my windows I can see the trees
The wind gently rocking the branches and leaves
'Neath the blue of the sky, the freshness of air
Is it God speaking?

The garden below with its shrubs and flowers
The late summer blooms that cheer the hours
The roses and petals that cover the ground.
Is it God speaking?

He speaks to us in so many ways
If our ears are in tune to what he says
If we open our eyes to the things around.
Yes, it is God speaking.

The birds on the trees, in the branches are swaying
The trill of their songs, what are they saying?
Their joyful music of the chorus at dawn
Can you hear God speaking?

From the smallest flower, to the tallest tree
We thank our God for eyes to see
The whole creation are the works of His hand
Mountains and valleys of every land.
So deep and great no rule can measure
His love for us, so great a treasure
So come alive to the sound of His voice
Because He is saying rejoice, rejoice,
Be happy my children, in all He has given
This earth of ours is the stairway to heaven.

Kathleen McQueen

A Walk By The Canal

A walk by the canal just you and me
peering over the bridge, what can we see?
An orange float and the hook is baited
in silence we watched and waited
circular ripples glisten in the sun
as fish dart about one by one.
The line tightened, it played hard to get.
Then a large trout was landed in a net.
Smiling the fisherman was full of glee
after weighing it, he set it free.
We walked down by the water side
to watch the lock gates open wide
a colourful barge glided through
well tanned owners bought their little dogs too
The lock had to fill to a level very high.
It is a pleasure to watch as they go by
a flash of a kingfisher and a blackbird sings.
There are dragonflies with gossamer wings.
Peace and quiet and breathing fresh air.
Enjoying the scenery and time to stare,
we sit on the seat placed on the grass
to greet the people as they pass.
Now it is time to be on our way
we will remember this lovely day
as pensioners now we don't need to spend,
our company we enjoy, with God as our friend.

R M Rawlings

HIS PROMISE

Sad what can be read in papers!
Or even what can be heard on the news
It can really upset and depress you!
Sometimes, it's so bad it can give you the blues.

But then those stories of evil,
Have been in the headlines before
Behind, are good people (who in secret)
Do deeds, appreciated a little, (no more).

Thank God for the light He keeps shining
Though the sadness, loss and pain.
For He is always there, when there is pining
Believe, and He will put peace in our hearts again.

E Morgan

GIFTS

O love, beyond all human understanding,
That holds the universe in single span,
Stoop down, give strength to all who seek the high road,
Envelop me.

O joy, such wondrous treasure granted to us,
Remain with us in all our lives to be.
Contain us as we travel onwards, praising,
Transfigure me.

O peace, essential constant of our journey,
Come, Holy Spirit, breath of life and power,
Give peace within, though all around is raging,
Encompass me.

Love, joy and peace, these gifts from God the Father,
Are ours by faith in Him, great One in Three.
Uphold us on our pilgrim way to Heaven,
O Trinity.

D Irvine

THE CONVENT

I wandered round the cloisters
Within those ancient walls
My thoughts went back to long ago
I fancied I heard calls.

So many feet have traversed
Along that well worn path
So many have found comfort
And peace of mind at last.

So many problems solved at length
After much serious thought
By prayer and meditation
And things that can't be bought.

I wander round the cloisters
Where all is quiet and still
Makes one to feel so humble
And try to do God's will.

A Kendall

In Such A Night As This

In such a night as this
Almighty God takes human flesh
to be vulnerable infancy

> In such a night as this
> he is saved from slaughter
> by the flight of refugees

In such a night as this
close to the end he gives himself
in food and drink to his friends

> In such a night as this
> he cries to God to remove the ordeal
> yet obeys his will

In such a night as this
he is betrayed by friends,
tortured and condemned to die

> In such a night as this
> Easter dawn explodes upon the earth
> breaking the spell of darkness:
> The Risen Lord fills creation
> with the new life, glory of his Love.

Angela Matheson

THE TREES

They swirled and danced flickering light and shade in my garden
        on a light and balmy day
To and fro they rustled delighting the birds, their life see sawing
        on the undulating bough
It was if an unseen orchestra was playing and they were moving
        to the strains of the music
Violins played in my garden and the trees were applauding to the
        mystic and the magic.
Came the night and the gentle taps on my window beckoning me to
        come and join them in the dance
The tapping became urgent, the wind howled and whined, but morpheus
        had me in his dreams
I dreamt that the sun and moon were going to kiss and the trees were
        trying to tell
Moments of magic, momentous moments would they really meet and
        the moon eclipse the sun.

G Graham

TO GOD

As another day closes and shadows fall
I find peace and am glad to be alone
To ponder on life and where I am going
To realise my failings and once more
Seek help and strength to carry on,
Down a path I hardly know,
With guidance from above, perhaps one day
I'll find that which I seek and
Humbly bend my knees and pray to God
To understand what I do not understand.

Liz Dicken

The Composer's Death

Lover of Johann Sebastian Bach's
Reflective chorales, that transmit moods
And interpret meaning of biblical themes,
After you and I had discussed my millennium poem,
You transformed my meditation into melody
And conducted the choir that first performed
The opening entreaty that rose to triumphant affirmation.

Little could we foresee that, so soon, and suddenly,
You would no longer be with us, and assembled here
On this radiant summer's day a congregation would gather
In thanksgiving service, with family tributes
And musical testimony to your abundant life.
Once again I sat and listened to your setting,
And knew your sharing of spirit in unbroken continuity.

J H Higginson

WHAT'S A POEM?

What's a poem?
a dream no less
not a verse?
yet it's more . . .

a soufflé turned out well?
Yet it's more . . .

a thrown-honed pot?
Glazed and fired to perfection
not a 'second'
yet it's more . . .

a new experience?
A shattering blow?
A chilling cold that
runs you through and through?
Yet it's more . . .

A coming together
in the reader's mind?
Yet it's more . . .

Some say it's a gift -
the first line perhaps?
Yet it's more . . .

A poem is a pearl?
But it's more . . .
It's more . . .

Richard Stoker

TO YOU LORD THE GLORY

Celebrate this great millennium, let's build a massive Dome,
no matter that some people have nowhere to call home.
Inside place many tributes, to achievements far and near,
though exploiting of resources has harmed the atmosphere.
The poor and sick are suffering for want of food to eat,
yet still we hoard in mountains lest stores we do deplete.
Scores of people dying from wars and bitter strife,
whilst the innocent are tortured and crime's so very rife.
The greedy and the grasping demand a monstrous fee
for working through the last hours of this twentieth century.
A bright new life before us . . . or just another day?
Two thousand years since Jesus was born to show the way.
His the only answer, His the truth to live.
Care about each other, for love we have to give.
For every single person whatever is their plight,
is made in God's own likeness, and justice is their right.
Jesus gave us talents and freedom in their use.
Apply them for all goodness, not derision or abuse.
So cast aside the notion that progress comes from man,
For Jesus is the Master, His the greatest plan.
If all would heed His message and hate and evil leave,
then truly could we celebrate, this December's new years Eve.

Cecilia Skudder

LIKE A CHILD

I want to be like a child where your love has set me free,
I want to be like a child Lord where your love has set me free.
Being in your loving arms Lord that's where I want to be.
Like a child you have set me free.

Catherine Can

THE NURSE IS

The nurse is only the nurse . . . and yet,
The nurse is . . . in a unique, special and humbling position.
The nurse is . . . by the nature of her position
        and proximity (and, we can even say intimacy,)
        to the patient, required to act sometimes
        'in loco parentis,'

    both to the young and old.

He or she may wield skills, words and tools
        to help or hinder the process of healing
        in the patient in his or her charge.
A cog, so to speak, in that healing process,
        not only physical, but sometimes
        emotional and psychological.

The nurse is not -

The nurse is not the doctor, nor the judge, not
        the priest, nor God!

Eleanor Thomas

UNTITLED

Faith my friend -
Believe that your prayers shall be answered.
Look not at the shadows that lay about you
But lift your eyes to the bright heavens.
Know that each burning star is as a prayer fulfilled,
And for every star you look upon
Ten thousand more burn unseen.

Steve Storey

THOSE BOOKS!

Oh, the delights of being able to read!
Enjoyment, relaxing, and blessings indeed.
To sit and to rest, with a nice cup of tea,
Would be good for you, and very good for me.
I soar in my mind, to countries far away,
And over mountains, on another day.
I sit by the sea, then float on my back,
Skies are blue and of sunshine there is no lack,
Then I read of countries where there's not much food,
And pray people will help them; that would be good.
I read of places where there is famine, bad,
Of children dying, that is so very sad.
Many of my books take me to happy days,
Of people, with God's help, teaching of His ways.
Then there are books of poems, helpful and wise,
Enlightening many, opening my eyes.
Others, comforting, when feeling down and sad,
Hope is given and we begin to feel glad.
Thank you God for all that write such helpful things,
Opening our minds, such wonderful thoughts to bring.
Oh, the happiness of reading a good book!
Sitting by the window, or a cosy nook.
May our reading matter be good for our eyes
And authors be guided to write what is wise!

Lilian Loftus

Vandalism

The church windows were smashed in St Mary's today
We wondered by whom as we knelt down to pray.
And why, for what reason, the damage was done
In this place of peace where we met with God's son.

We thought about you, and as we were kneeling
Our thoughts were alive with what you might be feeling.
What brought about your actions, what was in your mind
What vent for your emotions did you think you might find?

What was it you hoped that you might find there
For of monetary value our Church is bare.
But riches it holds in the welcome you'd find
If you came through the door with an open mind.

For no matter your troubles God understands
And he'll reach out to you with forgiving hands.
Take to him your problems, the anger you feel
Give it all to Him and ask him to heal.

Beryl Wagner

MORNING

Sack grey day,
Baggy clouds loosely shroud
the land.
The sweet soaked smell
Of sod and turf
bark and beach
and then, such is the beauty of our skies,
Like a promise kept
Our sun arrives
Broadly beaming
Warming, healing
Morning has broken.

Clair Green

A Plea

Come back to me my child
I died on the cross for thee,
Give up your wanderings wild
I died to set you free.
Once you walked so close
The world had lost its hold
It was the Christian way you chose
On the path to the city of gold.
Oh, child be not deceived
The world cannot give you peace
'Twas when you first believed
I gave you sweet release.

Doris Riley

THE TREE

The most precious tree of all the trees
is not the Christmas tree with tinsel baubles
And fairy lights adorned

It's not the tree who's laden blossom fills
The air with fragrance, making the senses reel
With pleasure sweet

Nor the greenest or the tallest tree
Nor the autumn tree with coloured leaves
Such beauty displaying

No not one of these no leaves or blossom
Cut down one task to perform to become the cross
Jesus carried to Calvary

Then nailed to the cross His blood and sweat stained
The most precious tree on which He son of God
Died for humility

M Hunter

ALWAYS! REMEMBER!

Never, pronounce them dead, who peacefully sleep
With fateful smile and divine peace you silently weep
Once their tasks on earth are wholly done
The supreme Father uniquely welcomes them home

Do not mourn their absence a great loss
Their second journey starts the moment they went across
All fertile seeds sown in spirit filled directions
Will display their last words, deeds and actions.

God's love for us, we will never comprehend
Considering all aspects, He is the beginning and the end
Yet He sacrificed His only begotten Son
As ransom for despicable deeds we have done.

Always! Remember Jesus filled times spent together
And in simplicity God's love shared with each other
Though they are separated from all earthly trends
We ought, to strive as significant loved ones, family and friends

With the supreme Father's name forever glorified
By whose divine grace we are purely sanctified
We are divinely equipped and set apart
To labour in fields visibly touching human heart.

Stay blessed.

E Coke

ODE TO A DEAD DOG

I remember when I saw you, rolling in the grass
On a day that God made lovely, through the power of the sun
And in my eyes you shone, as a perfect friend to man
I admired so your vitality, as round and round you ran.

For three seasons you had lived through, autumn, summer, spring,
Then something unexpected came to cut short your winter days
Now God grants you pure tranquillity as you lie at rest
But I am grateful that I saw you, when you were at your best.

A E Fox

A Holiday In Wales

What more can one hope to find
Than love of friends, and peace of mind
The majesty of mountains, the beauty of vales
All these one finds in tranquil Wales.

The changing vistas day by day
As waves wash gently cross the bay
Whipped up by winds,
Warmed by the sun
Changing in colour as day is done.

Children play on golden sand
Building castles firm and strong.
The old stone forts still guard the land
Their walls have stood for ages long.
But stronger than all human hands
Rain, storms and tides all come and go.
Forts of stone, or castles of sand
Are laid down low.

Nan Gosling

I Believe, I Believe, I Believe

I believe, I believe, I believe in Jesus Christ.
I believe He is the son of God
I believe in Him.

I believe, I believe, I believe in the blood of the lamb
The forgiveness of sins and eternal life,
I believe in Him.

I believe, I believe, I believe He gave His life,
On the cross at Calvary
I believe He died for me
Showing His love for eternity
I believe in Him.

I believe, I believe, I believe in the peace of God,
In His faithfulness and righteousness
Mercy, grace and radiance,
I believe in Him.

I believe, I believe, I believe, the power of the blood,
Death and hell has lost its strife,
I will go from life to life,
I believe in Jesus Christ
Yes I believe in Him.

Barbara Smith

THE TRUTH WILL SET YOU FREE

'It's a sin to tell a lie,' old crooners used to sing,
Yes, to tell a lie is quite a dreadful thing,
So always tell the truth, an honest person be,
Because you know, the truth it sets you free.

The first lie told to Eve, it caused a lot of strife,
Brought untold anguish to Adam and his wife,
Mankind in bondage to sin, held in captivity,
Until the day that Jesus, brought the truth to set men free.

'I bear witness to the truth' said Jesus to the Governor of the land,
'What is truth?' asked Pilate, he didn't understand,
And so on a cross our Lord, He died in agony,
The truth of which, from sin has set us free.

He rose and then ascended, to His throne on high,
His victory it has broken, the power of the lie,
In heaven now, He intercedes for you and me,
And so the truth of Jesus, is the truth that sets us free.

'Tell the truth and shame the devil,' so they say,
Why tell a lie, do you want to make his day?
Only to the Lord, make sure you bow the knee,
And then you'll find, the truth will set you free.

Jesus' sacrifice, our sins has washed away,
No more the price of sin, we have to pay,
Soon Jesus will return, and every eye will see,
This is the truth, that surely sets us free.

Pauline Wilkins

ARE YOU WILLING?

Are you willing to pick up your cross,
To pray for the dying, sick and the lost,
To give bread to the hungry
And clothes to the poor?
Are you really willing to give them your all?

For without God you can do nothing
For He is the great I am
We need to bow the knee and cry
And say 'Yes Lord' here am I.

S Sanders

THE HOLY SPIRIT

At Pentecost, God gave a gift
To those who gathered there,
He sent His Holy Spirit -
A great noise filled the air.
Men spoke in many languages
The spirit gave them power,
Such wonder and amazement grew
In that Pentecostal hour.
Some said that maybe they were drunk
But Peter made it plain,
He quoted Joel's prophecy
That our Lord would come again.

Anne Smith

LIFE'S PASSING

I'm walking the pathways in the gardens in Heaven
Just as I used to do there on the earth
I smell the flowers soft fragrance so sweet
And see verdant green of the lawns so neat.

My life was happy and busy too
But I grew tired and had to leave
Now I am strong and healthy again
My work on earth was complete.

I was sad to go and leave behind
All those I held most dear
For I was fulfilled and life was great
Till ill health took the hand of fate.

Grieve not for me for I'm happy here
And the pain that I had is all gone.
In your memories of me I can ever be
For in those my life can go on.

B Johnson

FRIENDSHIP

When days are long and things go wrong,
And nothing seems to blend,
It's nice to know those hidden fears
Can be shared and halved with a friend.

Not only in times of laughter and joy,
But in the hour of sadness and tears
Affection linked between the two,
Sealed throughout the years.

Friendship's a very special thing,
It cannot be bought or sold
And worries no matter how heavy they are,
To a special friend are told.

So never forget in a quieter moment,
To mention them in a prayer,
Because to you they mean so much,
For your very life they share.

Kathleen Jay

WITH GOD BY YOUR SIDE

With God by your side
You're never alone
He shares his love with you
And makes it your own.
With God by your side
You're never afraid.
He gives you his courage
So happy you prayed.
With God by your side
What a joy life will be
He makes it a pleasure
Just try it and see.

R Dilks

THE SORROWFUL PASSION

For obedience to God's will,
By the suffering in delay, in the waiting and sweating,
Lonely isolation the misery, by remembering,
By doubting, the consideration of other's guilt,
The sheer enormity of the task, with human frailty,
The cost of forgiveness, achieved through betrayal.

Acute suffering, more weakening,
Insult and derision, lashes and whippings,
Cruel lacerations, another slap in the face,
Another stage, another trial, more of the price,
For our mercy, that He came to pay.

True humiliation, subjugation and mockery,
Setting the seal, made to look a fool,
A fool for God's sake, a fool for our sake,
Testing His endurance, nearing the limit.

Shouldering the weight, of all the sin,
Of the world, throughout all time,
Being the ransom, to attain our release,
Falling, not failing, for our faults,
Clearly bearing the burden, heaving and sighing.

A lone final sacrifice, all of the price,
Fulfilling the offering, that He came to give,
Final true atonement, by victory in loss,
Dying to live, dying to love, dying to show,
In Him the supremacy, of God's love.

John Atherton

A DAY AMIDST NATURE

Awoken to a cock crowing
A bleat of a sheep, a cow mooing
The dew upon the grass glistening in the sun
I thank the Lord for this dawn
The fragrance of flowers in bloom
Fills my nostrils in the room
The rush of the sea upon the shore
Where God said come hither no more
The white crystals of the sand sift through my fingers
The cry of the sea gulls lingers
The palm trees swaying gently in the breeze
Fruits on the trees crying eat me please!
Or that's the way I see
The sun rays beating upon my head
A dip in the sea cools the heat, before going red
Coconut water quench the thirst
Let's see who can finish first!
Flying fish and cou-cou, the dish of the day
The flies I shoo, leave my food I pray
The sun began to sink beyond the horizon
The colours and beauty fires the imagination
Mosquitoes took their share of bites
Upon my flesh, now it is nearing night
The deep dark blue of the sky
Amidst a few clouds the stars start peeping out
I got down on my knees to pray
Thanking God for the day He had made
And for the table He had laid
The mansion for which He had prepared
For the glory in heaven cannot be compared.

Deborah Thompson

WE CANNOT KNOW

We cannot know,
We cannot tell,
How our lives,
Will change things.

Have we accomplished,
What God desires,
To touch another's life?

Who it is,
Why, we must speak?
We, may never know,
This side of heaven.

We should somehow,
Show Christ
Within our lives,
To plant a seed of faith.

The choice to choose,
Is theirs alone,
We are but tools,
God can use,
To plant their feet,
On the road to faith.

Rita Hillier

REDEEM

Redemption hangs like a tattered scarf from some oil painting
A master's depiction of the Saviour
Dying on the cross of material hopes

All done for the spirit
All done in the spirit
All done to the spirit

And the redeemer hangs, nails with rust
Scratch into the nails on His hands
And the halo blooms
With a thousand, thousand, thousand
Prayers for forgiveness

And the unrepentant stare up
Empty mouthed or swallow another tablet
And turn their sights to the west
Convivial place where all men's hopes sink

Turning to the east
Another lamb bleats
Azreal and Israel
And the unstable multitudes
Wrap their heads in blood soaked swatches
And lighten up into the nothingness
Which is their destiny

Stained and scarred
The museum man
Unwraps the burdens of Egypt
Points and signs
And lets fall the precious last beetle:
That scarab reclining folds wings about the heads of dead pariahs.

And remember Jesus of Nazareth was in Egypt too.

Joy Sheridan

INSPIRATION

And in the fullness of time
All things shall be revealed
And the children that dwell in darkness
Shall awake and walk in the light.
And prayers said in the darkest of night
Shall be answered once more in the
Brilliance of the light.

Lucille Norton-Ercan

PILGRIM'S REGRESS

Hello, said the pilgrim to those who could not hear
But the tremble in his voice gave away his fear
.He pushed through the door and on down the hall
Blissful, unaware, riding for a fall
For the house was built across a well
Which ferried souls between Heaven and Hell
And far away in the celestial dark
God and the Devil watched him as a spark
God shrugged, on sunbeams he was up to speed
But a spirit like that the Devil had a need
So Satan smiled at the pilgrim's frown
He touched his soul and he took him down.

Douglas Lawrie

EVENING

Outside, the setting sun is sinking fast,
A ball of iridescent red;
The rush of yet another day is past
And now the crowded marts are dead.

Back at the office, all at last is still;
No longer rings the busy phone;
Gone are the workers, silent is the mill,
And all the farming hands are home.

Full soon, the last few reddish streaks of day
Have gone from sight beyond the west
And creatures of the night must seek their prey
While man would turn aside for rest.

And yet how oft, when evening shades grew deep,
When past was one more tiring day,
My Lord would leave His followers in sleep
To find a lonely place to pray.

There, 'neath the olive trees His hands had made,
With ne'er a pillow save the sod,
There, in the very place He was betrayed,
He kept His secret tryst with God.

And if my Saviour felt the need of strength
Enough to spend all night in prayer,
How much the more need I to pray at length
My Father's will to know and share?

So, as I look back o'er the closing day,
Its chances now for ever past,
I ask myself, *'Just how much did you pray,
That what you've done today might last?'*

Robert A Hardwidge

PRISONER'S PRAYER

Jesus loves a sinner,
That means me and you.
Although you're in a prison cell,
The Lord will see you through.

Let him know you love him,
Let him know you care
And if you look outside your cell
You'll find him standing there.

All the pain and worry
That you're going through,
When the master walked this land,
He went through it too.

So look in to your heart today
And praise the Saviour's name,
Ask him to forgive you
And your life won't be the same.

Jamesie Gardner

I Pray

Lord above who helps the sick,
Can you please help my brother Dick?
He has been ill ever since July,
In *intensive care*, I thought I'd die!
The doctors are doing all they can,
They have, since the illness first began.
But with your help, I'm very sure
Their treatment will produce a cure.
I pray each night and daytime too
For more assistance Lord, from you.
A miracle is what we need,
I pray for this Lord, please take heed.

Margaret Rankin

TINSEL ON THE XMAS TREE

A cave Mary and Joseph saw
To shelter with their babe
The winter frost shone all around
The babe they tried to save
From Herod's men a king to be
The Son of God to set us free.

A tiny spider found that cave
Tho' soldiers still did seek
From the small body spun a web
The spider could not speak
Of Herod's men come near to kill
The babe must do His Father's will.

The spider's web closed up the cave
With sparkling frost it shone
Unbroken so the soldiers saw
Turned round and then were gone
Put tinsel round the Xmas tree
A frosted spider's web you'll see.

M Hudson

CONFIDENCE

It is better to trust than to doubt,
For hope dulls the dart of despair,
The head knows what the heart is about -
Weighed down or elated through prayers.

Trust dwells in a garden of roses
With buds infinite 'round the gate.
The motto of confidence ever is:
'Write your name on God's Heart and wait!'

Lily H O'Reilly

TO THE UTTERMOST JESUS SAVES

Jesus save to the uttermost . . . This means just what it says,
Nothing's too hard for the Lord, from drugs' foul hell He saves.
.From beasts and scorpions of the pit He'll bring you forth, remember it.
He saves . . . Yes . . .! *Jesus saves!*

Challenge now our Saviour God and take Him up upon His word.
Call upon Him, '*Are* you there? Then save this sinner from my fear!
Jesus! Is it true, God's Son, pleading now for everyone
Who dares to claim His grace, *seek* His face . . . Repent?

Give your crushed heart *to God!* Ask *Him* to do the job aright,
To enter in its foul domain, clean it and then sit there to reign
As King on your heart's throne. He'll free it from each sinful chain
stop in a day the blinding pain, then *gently* make it whole again,
He saves - Yes! *Jesus saves.*
Challenge the Father thus I say:- 'God *is* your son alive today?
Show me, so I'll know, for . . . I am lost.'

Down from the holies you will find Peace comes to your tortured mind,
And should you go to seek your sin, the 'Sentinel' *will not let it in!*
Inside your heart . . . (this might *seem* odd) will be the Spirit
                                              of Jesus -*God*
Who hates and quite subdues all ill and after that you nevermore will
love the evil things.

Christ in us . . . *that* is the glory of the wondrous Gospel story,
And instead of being a sinful sod, you're *'born again'* a Son of God.

Rose Culley

The Valley Of The Shadow

Deep in my mind
there is a valley,
shadowed by the
uncertainty of coming night,
before the stars give
their light and guidance.

Maybe I fear what I may lose
in the valley's maze of ageing?
Yet all I have to do is choose
to breathe the sacred breath,
taking each step thankfully.

Life achieved,
life given and received
in an abundance of
tender loving care.

Anne Smith

THE PREACHER

Sometimes alas, we may not know
Through difficulty he must go
In studying the word of God
Or, following in paths well trod.
In dealing with the Church's need
And, on his knees he has to plead.
In going on that *extra mile*
Whilst trying to maintain a smile,
When meeting folk who do not care
And, even brethren stand and stare
When, in a lonely path he goes,
Quite unaware of grief and woes
Then, at the service he must share
His thoughts with sympathetic care
And love, as joy and peace accord
With blessing from our Saviour, Lord.
To encourage, when satanic power
Would seek to take away, devour
The word so feelingly set forth
So priceless and of matchless worth.
Pray for The Preacher every day;
That God sustains in all the way
The Preacher goes, throughout his life,
And keep him in the stress and strife.

Fred Hill

LIVE WITHIN MY HEART

Dear Jesus above, guard the paths I walk,
Prayers said in mime, for I cannot talk.
No words of love, from my lips depart.
I may not speak, words of love fill my heart.

In my heart I feel the comfort of you.
Your love from Heaven is given so true.
You guide me through my troubles each day.
My heart carries, loving words I want to say.

Love within my heart, you are welcome there.
Love from angels above, shows someone cares.
Your world around me, it's true I cannot see.
But I know you live within the heart of me.

I don't need pity, when you walk by my side.
In your loving world, I have no need to hide.
You are the way, the way I always want to go.
I will walk the path of Jesus, my life will grow.

Though I cannot see, you guard the roads I walk
You always hear my words, though I cannot talk
While you live in my heart, I will never know sorrow.
For I know, you will walk, by my side tomorrow.

Kevin P S Collins

CHANGING

The sun is shining, oh happy day
People are smiling, children play.
With sky of blue and clouds fluffy and white,
Oh lovely hours, passing through to night.

Today it's raining, oh what a change.
It's colder now and the fire's in the range.
Leaves are falling, summer's past,
Autumn's here, winter coming on fast.

We see God's work in all its glory,
As gold leaves and red and brown
Telling the Bible's story
With God's presence all around.

Then let us put our hands together,
Tell the Lord we understand
Why the different types of weather
Go together, hand in hand.

Don Friar

QUESTIONS?

A moment of time is two thousand years
Since Christ walked this earth among men,
What was life like when He was a babe
Is it now better than then?

How have we done in two thousand years?
Some would say really well,
While others would say we've made a right mess,
And are sending our souls straight to hell.

What have we done in two thousand years?
Some would say quite a lot,
While others would say more harm than good,
And deserve all the problems we've got.

What have they brought, those two thousand years?
Some would say wonders galore,
While others would say more pain than gain,
Cruelty, poverty and war.

What must God think of those two thousand years,
Is He angry, or pleased with His flock?
Are we just sinking in dark soggy mire,
Or are we all standing on rock?

'God is working His purpose out'
I sang in a hymn when a child.
So maybe we're living the way that He planned,
On this world He created so wild.

And if God is weaving His pattern,
My actions I hopefully pray,
Are the threads He decides should be woven
In lovely bright colours - not grey!

Avis Ciceri

ONE SLEEPLESS NIGHT

No stars above . . . no sign of a moon
    Not even a glimmer of light
As I opened my window . . . to look out into the world
    On another sleepless night.

Sky was grey . . . nothing stirred
    Not even my apple tree
As I stare from my window . . . into the night
    As far as I could see.

A train in the distance . . . rumbled thru;
    What mysteries did it hide
Was that a rustle or a whispered word
    Was there someone in the dark outside.

I am alone . . . night is long
    No one to hold me tight
I must go back to my bed again
    And pray for the morning light.

Gwen Tominey

CHRIST CHILD 2000

An innkeeper was charged for
Allowing a woman to give birth
In a stable alongside oxen and ass
Said he was being charitable.
Would you believe it?

Some shepherds were arraigned for
Leading their lambs right into the town.
Thought to be a protest against low prices
Said they were called by some angels.
Would you believe it?

Three men were deported for
Trying to cross frontiers, but without
Passports they looked like illegal immigrants.
Said they were following a great star.
Would you believe it?

Police went to seize parents
For keeping a Babe in a manger
And evading the Social Services
But they had fled southwards together.
Would *you* believe it?

C Morris

Two Thousand Years

Two thousand years since our Lord was born,
Two thousand years since that happy morn.
God looked down on a sinful world
He thought what can I do to set them free,
To cleanse them fit to be my family.
I cannot live with them in their sinful state,
I will send someone I love to put them right.
I will send my son to shed his blood,
To make them clean to live with me,
To be my own beloved family.

On that cross so long ago
Jesus died in agony, to put us right in God's sight.
He took all our sins and woes,
Obeyed his father and suffered there,
That we might at last be fit to go,
To live with our Father in His Heavenly abode.

Ena Stanmore

HOLINESS DIVINE

Praises sing for our Saviour king
he's with us everywhere.
In our hearts such wonderful love
fruits of the spirit to share.

Joy, peace and hope then to impart
grace for the trials to see.
Guide with your perpetual light
by our side eternally.

Protect us Lord where're we be
courage for each new day.
Restore our strength, such faith bestow,
safe in your arms alway.

With grateful thanks rejoice be glad
in your glory to shine.
So we may share your wine and bread
such holiness divine.

Margaret Jackson

WORTHY TO BE PRAISED

The Lord who made the heavens and the earth
The stars that shine, the sunset and the sea
Is wonderful and worthy to be praised
Because He also cares for you and me.

'Let not your hearts be troubled,' and 'Be not afraid,'
He's Father, Saviour, friend and brother too.
He loves and knows each one of us so well
And came to earth and died for me and you.

The powerful Creator Father God
Holds us in the hollow of His hand,
If we trust Him for everything in life
He'll take us with Him to the Promised Land.

Joan Marsh

DAY SIX

A world bathed in darkness,
Only the moon and stars for company.
All is silent, all is still.
Perfect peace, perfect harmony.

A chink of light shows on the horizon,
Heralding the dawn of a new day
The sun ascends, throwing back the cloak of darkness
Letting the colours of creation now have their say.

A river meandering along a winding course
Its clear blue water sparkling, fresh and bright.
The fish swim in the rivers and dance in the seas
Going about their lives unhindered, out of sight.

The only sound is that of the wind
Whistling its way through the trees,
The birds make no noise as they soar high in the sky
Gliding effortlessly along on a gentle breeze.

The grass is green, the trees grow tall
Flowers open bursting into colour again.
All of them renewed and revitalised
By a light thirst quenching rain.

As the day carries on, animals appear
Exploring their world, a first day to savour.
Everywhere they go is a new place to them
Everything they eat a new taste, a new flavour.

And as the world moves through day six
Purity and peace spread throughout the land
Surely this flawless genesis will remain as it is
In this world as yet untouched by human hands.

David Lord

Journey's End

When Mary and Joseph to Bethlehem came
Seeking shelter from the cold
Where're they asked it was the same
'You can't sleep here' they were told.

The town was full, it seemed to be.
People returned home by land
To be taxed by some decree
Caesar Augustus had planned.

A lowly stable was all to be had.
For no more could Mary roam.
And though at times she would feel sad,
She had to make this home.

When Jesus was born in that stall,
It was a special night
Ox and ass would before him fall.
Around his head was light.

Carolyn M Sill

To Mother - 1975

This verse is just a little token,
My real words remain unspoken.
What can I say about you Mum!
I'm really grateful for all you've done.
Through the passing of the years
You've shared all my hopes, and fears.
With loving guidance you've stood by
I don't need to ask you 'Why?'
The answer's plain for all to see.
For you're the best mum there could be!

Celia Ann Islam

When Sunday Comes

There was a time that I recall
When on Saturday I'd have a ball
Staying out beyond the night
With blood-shot eyes in morning light

My friends and I would form a line
And guzzle down our jugs of wine
Places gone and people seen
Could not remember where I'd been

Sunday morning bleary eyed
Amazed again I had survived
With a head of pain and a mouth so dry
I'd look in the mirror and demand to know why

But now thank God the times have changed
The difference in me across the range
For when Saturday was a quick thrill gone
Now it's a prelude to when Sunday comes

M Milliken

HAND POWER

Summer time - winter time
                        just by the hour
O' the hands of the clock
                        have magnificent power
For the darkness arrived - that much
                        sooner tonight
Just by one - motion - gone
                        summer's light!
Illuminated illusion - or next
                        morn's confusion
Or winter time!

O' the hands of the clock have
                        magnificent power
Ruling our lives - by its hour
                        by hour
Seasons and reasons - and people
                        can alter
But not for one moment -
                        hands of time falter
Yet - Almighty the hands - that
                        rule this great power
Mighty and mystic
                        Hour - by hour.

Rita White

THE WISEMEN

Kings from the east
Travelled afar.
Weary camels
Followed the star.
Herod told them
Of a new king,
'Find him quickly
And then return
Safely to me.'
The Wisemen thought,
And then they sought.
Found history
What a story!
The first gave gold
He was so bold.
Next Frankincense
That made real sense.
The third gave Myrrh
World of treasure.
Then returning
Another way
So they say now.
Kings from the east
Travelled afar.
Weary camels
Bowed to the star.

Valerie Kirwood Edwards

HE KNOWS THE CROSS WE HAVE TO BEAR

(For we through the spirit by faith wait for hope of righteousness) Gal 5:5

God has a time for each role He appoints
May we always wait for His lead.
Dwell not on the density of the fog,
Just continue to sow the good seed.

Such sweet whisperings of His wondrous love
Are held in the heart that believes.
Well He knows the cross we have to bear
And is aware when the Spirit grieves.

A little love and the hand of forgiveness
Will help this old world along.
A word of cheer often drowns a fear
Just one note can start a song.

Though, He cannot comfort Your distrust
So smile and keep Your armour bright.
Even the fairest flower has its shadow beneath it
As it swings in the sunlight.

Doreen Craig

IN YOU WE TRUST

To hear of your word Lord, its peace be, for me
Its parable stories, thoughts of which you'd agree.
In verses of stories, in places, domain,
In phrases of glories, of you good to acclaim.
The praises tomorrow, it raises today
In needing to borrow, its praises to pray.
At heart of all heartfelt, at peace with ones own,
Its peace-ments are in-dwelt, in centre be sown
In fingers of digits, in hands that reach too
In reaching of attainment, in songs that are true.
Tomorrow, today then, was yesterday's place,
In hands that are in reach of, in God's, so his grace.
So life it is onwards, its shores we look here,
Its sand's ever changing, it's dunes are of clear,
The sprinkled grain sand of, the tide so it goes
Its ebbings and goings, it outwardly shows.
We wade through with bare feet, the water's so clear,
It covers the oceans, the seas of good cheer.
We are so, but human, and cannot but see,
That our life here on earth is, laid out from thee.
For when it is gone through, and troubles do come,
Have strength in God's presence, trust, peace, everyone.

Hugh Campbell

Keep A Watch On Your Words

Let us be careful of the words that we say
for words can be cruel
and words can be kind,
they can cut to the bone
like a two-edged knife
they can comfort a troubled mind.
Refrain if the words are cruel
once said like a bullet they're gone
the wound, it sometimes never heals
and healing can be slow and long,
they may flash through your mind like lightning,
don't say them as quick as they strike
then you won't be sorry tomorrow,
for words that are spoken
in moments of spite.
Let your words be spoken
with fairness and truth
may peace and love guard your mind
your life will be a much happier place
and your words be honest and kind.

Frank Scott

DON'T WORRY RAP

Why do you worry?
Why should you care?
What to eat?
What to wear?

There's *more* to life
Than clothes or food!
Worry will *never*
Do any good!

Look at the birds in the sky . . .
Hear them sing,
Watch them fly.
They don't fret,
Slog or store.
Yes! God loves them:
But He loves *you* more!

Look at the plants with lovely flowers on -
Think of the story of King Solomon!
In all his glory, he was brightly arrayed,
But never as brightly as the flowers God made!

Trust in God!
Just live today!
Give Him tomorrow -
He'll clear your way!
Forget your own wants . . .
Seek first God's will!
He's promised to care for you:
He always will!

Heather M Simpson

Spring's Awakening

Spring is a time for awakening growth
when the earth comes alive after sleep,
Buds appear on the bare naked limbs of trees,
and shoots from the earth do peep.
Pussy Willows bear catkins resembling chicks,
Crocus bloom amid fallen bricks.
Snowdrops glisten with snowy white,
They sprinkle the ground with frosty light.
Nodding heads like bells that chime
Springs own messengers, time after time.

Primroses shyly take a peek,
From under hedges, fresh and sweet.
Ferns unfurl their fronds of green,
Asleep for winter they have been.
Now they wake, brown furled and shy,
Point their fingers to the sky.
Soon the bluebells growing free,
Spread a blue hued carpet like the sea
Wave their heads in rippling rows,
like sea waves on a Galley's bows.
Foxgloves point their spears on high,
basking upward to the sky.
The yellow gorse in patches bold,
lends to the hedges tones of gold.
Spring is a time of colour and hope
from the country lanes to the mountain slope.
Let us enjoy it, too soon it is gone,
and another season has begun.

Isobel Laffin

Approaching The Twenty-First Century

It is August nineteen ninety nine,
Only four more months to go;
Until the year two thousand,
Then this century will be no more.

I wonder what the Millennium will bring!
Will we discover what are UFOs?
Will there be more astounding inventions?
Will the whole world change radically so?

Only time will reveal all,
As we cannot really foresee!
We can but pray it will be for the better,
And more people will live in harmony . . .

June Legg

The Gospel According To You

Is there a God? You may well ask -
does he live out there in space?
To find *Him* is no major task,
for he is one of the *human race*.
He is a creation in the mind of man,
seeking a *symbol* of the human ideal,
founded on memories of those we love,
there in everything that we see and feel.

The satisfaction of knowing a job is well done, all those
little good things in life, the feeling you get when a battle
has been won, dealing with all the trouble and strife,
you will find Him anywhere that you may be, beside you
when there is a family tragedy, the refreshment of a
good night's sleep, a comfort when your grief is deep.

Daily miracles of the world around us, the greetings of the
birds in the dawn chorus, the sun shining through the mist
in the early morning, promising that a glorious day is dawning,
a luscious green valley where a clear river flows, on a mountain
top when a strong wind blows, hedgerows covered with the wild
pink rose, tranquil meadows filled with bluebells and primrose.

Green grass gleaming with the morning dew, an abundance
of colourful flowers in spring, a feeling of joy when a blackbird
sings, the warmth of the sun setting your heart aglow, the dark
red sky heralding a sunset glare, a touch of frost in the evening
air, starlings returning home to their nest, the shriek of their calls,
as dusk creeps in and the darkness falls.

Create a God from the good that comes your way,
the innocence of children, the joy of a wedding day,
a heart flowing with thoughts that are honest and true,
it's where you'll find Him, to help you through.

Robert Gerald

JOYOUS TIMES

Nineteen ninety nine saw the eclipse.
What a fete - everything goes black
when sun and moon meet the light
comes shining through making everything
look like new.

Then the year two thousand will be a memorable year
with many celebrations, and plenty of cheer.
God willing my husband and I will see
our fiftieth Golden Wedding Anniversary.

They've built a Dome what a lovely sight
to mark the millennium that's vast and bright.
But lakes and snow-capped mountains are so grand
there's nought to compare with God's natural land.

What wondrous things in nature there are
that God has created both near and far.
We should thank the good Lord above
for all these blessing He gives with love.

Elizabeth M Dowler

TEARS OF PEACE

The whimpering, mewing soul,
of this fresh-born child,
trembles at the trumpeting march
of triumphs past.
This sinew'd infant; fashioned
by fear,
and shaped by the Jerico'd horn
of Old Nick's rasp,
weeps with the faltering pride
of peace.
He is lulled by grief's sweet
smelling breath.
This sinew'd child, born of a
nation's tune of hope,
reincarnated by a land that rejoices
in the joy of death!
'Oh please' we hear its people sigh,
'with tears of peace let
bloody Belfast cry!'

Bryon J Jones

POPE JOHN PAUL PAID A VISIT
(Cardiff - 2nd June 1982)

Beneath the rising sun at break of day
The altar bathed in early sunshine ray.
We gathered in our thousands on the sward
To listen to the servant of our Lord.
We travelled thro' the night from near and far
By train, by bus and cherished family car.
The aged, the young, the fit and the ill
Came to receive a message of goodwill.
What a joy this has been
To be a part of life's tapestry's scene
I moved away contented and fulfilled
Another one of life's ambitions, thrilled.

F N Fairchild

THE YEAR OF OUR LORD 2000

In the year of our Lord 2000
What will the future bring?
More trouble, strife and cruelty,
Or a world fit for a king!

I was born before the twenties,
And had much time for thought.
About events through all those years,
And the battles that we fought.

I remember too, the blessings,
And give thanks for every boon.
The conquering of Everest!
The walking on the Moon!

Radio and movies,
Telephone and TV.
The fridge and central heating,
Microwave and instant tea.

What would I wish for the future?
A world of sweet accord!
Oh! What could be more wonderful,
Than the coming of the Lord?

Marjorie Jones

The Christmas Season

When the north wind blows it brings the snow
it falls in the valley below.
There is a chill in the air and a nip, Jack Frost is everywhere.
The trees are bare, and covered in snow
the robin sits on the bough, he is our feathered friend
and visits us each year
when we see him we know that winter is here.
He picks up the scattered berries that fall upon the ground,
the wind blows and the leaves lie around
the snow has covered all the ground.
This is a time for children to light up the Christmas tree
to see the candles glow and to stand beneath the Mistletoe.
A kiss for you, and a kiss for me, and a kiss for Santa Clause,
this is the night he comes to town wearing his red dressing gown
and in his bag he's lots of toys all for little girls and boys.
He brings them dolls, and golliwogs, and big brown dancing bears,
to see their little face light up as he answers little prayers.
Then he quietly goes down stairs,
and with him he brings good cheer for a Merry Christmas
and a Happy New Year.
It's time for young and old to enjoy the festive season
and get together with old friends.
Rejoice, rejoice . . . and toast the Christmas Season.

Helen Manson

God's Love

I love God and He loves me,
He loves each one of us.
He loves so much He died for us
His death upon a cross.

In Heaven He reigns above
And there I'll see my Lord.
If you believe, you'll see Him too
And have eternal life.

For God forgives us all our sins
If we repent and try
To live a better life on earth
And love each other too.

Angela Kellie

GUARDIAN ANGEL

Oh happy the day
when you were born
a bright and beautiful
sunny morn.
A special angel
whispered to me
what a wonderful person
you would grow to be.

If you feel anxious
at any hour
think of this angel
he has might and power.
He was sent by God
from Heaven above
to enfold his wings round you
and protect you with love.

Doris Rowe

TO EVENTIDE

Darkness falls with wondrous peace
Birds end their search for food
Only owls their cry do release
As they seek in perpetual mood
Shadows make the quaintest shape
As man relaxes in a chair
After his toil throws away his cape
And watches the fire flare
Giving thanks for his rest
As he thinks of next day's work
How he'll manage it the best
He knows he cannot shirk.

R Large

THE MILLENNIUM MESSAGE

In front of us all lies a clean, fresh start -
A page of the future in which to take part.
How shall we tackle this chance that's ahead?
Think not of ourselves but of others instead!

Will there be smiles instead of tears?
Will there be peace instead of fears?
Will there be joys instead of woes?
Will there be friends instead of foes?

Each of us has a small part to play,
Improving and helping each in our own way -
With kindness and love, with friendship and care
Our world could be wonderful, prosperous and fair.

So let's get together, united in love
(I'm sure we'll get plenty of help from above).
We'll build a new world for our children to share
Full of peace, hope and joy with people who care.

Bessie Martin

MY BELIEF

I've always believed in Jesus
Nearly all of my life
When we're young
We don't listen
To how God affects our lives.

Now that I am older
I know the Lord's
With me every day
With all my troubles and worries
The Lord is here to stay.

To believe may not make life easier
Maybe that's hard to understand
But Jesus didn't have life easy
It was always full of strife
But he believed in God
His Father who would
Take Him from this life.

He now looks down from Heaven
To see what mistakes we make
There are certain paths
In this life
That we should or shouldn't take
So he looks down and sees us
With all the faults we have
I'm going to keep on trying
With this great faith I have.

Trisha Moreton

A Summer Stroll

I walked along the pathway
Keeping my feet from the grass
There was plenty of space for me to walk
For there was no one to pass
As I looked around I thought how welcome I was made
A lovely red rose nodded its head
And the leaves on the trees gave a courteous wave
And showed me their berries so red
What a delight to see so many flowers of richest hue
A beautiful sight on a summer's morn
No price to pay for it was free.

Helen Knott

BUILDING

Two thousand years of building,
Gladly, persistently building,
On foundations laid by Apostles,
With Jesus the chief corner-stone.

Stones gathered from all people
Gently shaped by the Master's hand.
Purifying and making holy,
Living stones in the Church of God.

They found peace in forgiveness,
Rejoiced in the love of the Lord.
Bringing hope to a world of sadness
Shared the joy of serving their Lord.

Some would silence the witness
Not heeding the good news proclaimed.
But words of light and life in Jesus
Still goes forth in the Spirit's power.

The building must continue,
Not ceasing 'til the end of time.
When the church triumphant, glorified,
Will enter the presence of God.

Elsie Birch

HEAVEN

Heaven it's said is way above
Beyond the clouds so blue
But I say Heaven is here below
In all the good we do.

Angels' wings are beautiful
Their voices sweet and clear
But they do not compare
With man's compassion while he's here.

Charity it's often said
Should always start at home
But would it not be better
To help someone alone?

It's good to love our family
Brother, sister, child and mate
But as we do should we forget
The stranger at the gate?

So let us do the good we can
In all the ways we know
To each and everyone we meet
And find our Heaven here below.

Margaret Turner

To Live Forever

Bang . . . Bang . . . Bang . . . Silence
Bang . . . Bang . . . Bang . . . Still silence!
As He did his duty
He turned our lives to beauty.

Pull . . . Pull . . . Pull
Up . . . Up . . . Up
Thud! With crushing blows it falls in place,
And we behold, perfect grace.

Searing pain, stretching, tearing,
Freedom pouring, mixed with sweat,
And yet he forgives his persecutors,
Forgives us all, the blood is let.

Gasp . . . Gasp . . . Gasp
Last breath taken, still no shout.
Mercy, forgiveness, poured upon us,
As that final sigh breathes out.

Down . . . Down . . . Down
Limp and lifeless,
Broken, beaten . . .
Not quite yet!
For the serpents sin cannot hold him.

Up . . . Up . . . Up
In life arose
To live forever, so we can join him,
For it was for us, all this he chose.

Glory, Glory,
Praise and wonder
Hail a glorious risen King,
God has freed us, to live forever,
Through this great awakening.

Soan Nixon-Smith

A Gift For Christmas

There is no gift that I could give
To those whose empty eyes deride
The wondrous gift, already given
At that first Christmastide.
No better gift, unless they see
That star above the stall
And hear the angel choir proclaim
That 'He' is Lord of all.
The earth goes on its wounded way
And mankind still must learn
That, far above, the morning star
Proclaims 'He will return'
And so my gift at Christmas time
Would be the chance to bring
Some ransomed soul in the light
As my best offering.
And if the Lord should smile and say
That I had done my part
In telling of this wondrous love
That glows within my heart.
Then I would be content to leave
This world, so full of fear and strife
And lay my offering at His feet
And take *His gift - eternal life.*

Barbara Ashworth

TREE SURGEON

Following a path
beside a tree-lined stream
on Maundy Thursday
reminded me of Jesus Christ,
our living-water saviour,
whose journey meant
His blood and water
dripping for us
from a rough-lined cross.

Robert D Shooter

GOD'S MILLENNIUM

The time is near to say goodbye
To the twentieth century
And face another era
Not knowing what will be

The world moves on so rapidly
With many things anew
Like technology, new currency
And 'What more can we do'?

It's easy to be swallowed up
Into a material race
And it's easy to concern ourselves
With what goes on in space.

But we must not forget the One
Who gave us life to come
And strive for love and work for peace
In God's millennium.

Joy Francis

GOODBYE MARGARET, GOODBYE STUART

We find 'Goodbye' is very hard to say,
We wish that you would stay, not go away
But life moves on for all of us and so
Accept our thanks in friendship as you go.
Be sure your time here will not go to waste,
It leaves us spiritually better placed;
Your prayers, your faith, your hospitality
Have made their mark upon each personality
Leaving within our hearts that precious leaven
Which rising, helps to lift our thoughts to Heaven.
So 'Thank you both'.

May you be blessed in all the future brings,
Be borne aloft on powerful eagles' wings;
Where'er you walk among those Derby peaks
Enjoy the glory God in nature speaks;
Lift up your prayers to Him and every saint
Restored from weariness, refreshed from faint.
Then give to others that which we received,
Include them in the tapestries you've weaved;
Remember us as we remember you
Discovering together all things new.
So 'God be with you both' is now our cry -
Not hard to say at all - 'Goodbye, goodbye'.

Tom Hicks

SONNET TO A MILLENNIUM HOPE

O let us not judge man by passing eye,
Those visions cruel inspired by nature's joke
.That limping gait or visage cast awry
All human faults that often mirth evoke.
O that ones basic self be clearly taken
To set the rule by which each man is rated
His secret values not to be forsaken
When at his end his span is sealed and dated.
God grant compassion to the pow'rs so vested,
That at this time His will shall all pervade,
To let each man by virtue then be tested
Without a hint of prejudice displayed.
Should there be error in this hope of mine,
Then prayer is vain, nor is the cross a sign.

Thomas H Woods

IN TROUBLED TIMES

In troubles times
Poetry sometimes rhymes,
As church bell chimes
Out of time.

In troubled times
Poetry occasionally rhymes,
As ivy tightly twines
Round time-worn tower.

In troubled times
Poetry rarely rhymes,
As preacher tries
To speak to broken souls.

In troubled times
Poetry rhymes not,
As man in back pew sighs
Dreams of might have been.

And preacher, man in pew,
Me and you;
Living, deceased,
Will be released;
Retired, expired, inspired,
Will all meet peace.

Then no more troubled times,
Poetry forever rhymes;
And all forlorn stand tall,
Fly on eagles' wings, and never ever fall.

Ian Squire

THE WORD

Thank you that the 'word' is God and that God gives life to all
He fashions human beings and creatures great and small;
God made the landscapes of our world, the oceans, rolling seas,
Rain to feed earth's mountain streams, sustaining flowers and trees.
Sun, providing warmth and daylight,
Moon and sparkling stars in dark night;
Every seasons work of arts,
Signifies predicted parts;
Spring ensues new life to start,
Summer warms the land and heart;
Autumn yields the harvest, then -
Winter chills we face again;
For life's plan to give man hope,
God sent His Son to help us cope;
Those who hear and those who heed,
Know that God supplies all need;
Believing as they learn His way -
Earning everlasting life some day;
They sing God's praise, they spread His word,
Never doubting that our Lord is heard;
For in the midst of two or three,
Amongst us there, our Lord will be;
In His house of prayer or wherever you please,
Alone - standing - walking - down on your knees;
Forever true, always near,
The loud, or whispered 'word' He'll hear.

Ivy Squires

UNTITLED
(Matthew 6 v 34 - 'Therefore do not worry about tomorrow for tomorrow will worry about its own things')

What's so different about today
Well it can't ever come again
Yesterday was yesterday
And today can't be the same

Turn your arguing into love
Don't be afraid to say you're sorry
The ones you love are here today
But only God knows about tomorrow

Make every word and minute count
Don't wait until tomorrow
The time we have is here and now
It's not something we can borrow

So what's different about today
Well it can't ever come again
Yesterday was yesterday
And today won't be the same

Ann Langley

A New Beginning

Each year 'God' renews the earth
Making all things new
What's dead is then
Restored to life
To restart life anew
Let's make this great millennium year
A new start
For everyone
Everything clean
Shining bright
A joy for years to come.

Olwen Counsell

PRAYER FOR RADAR

We stood around that shallow grave
   Where soon would rest our friend.
Our tears gave way to hefty sobs
   His loss did us offend.
We found him lying in the yard,
   His body still and warm,
But life had left those smiling eyes
   To lend us all to mourn.
No more his ears would turn for sound
   Of those who brought his food;
Nor would he wrinkle up his nose
   As carrot skins he chewed.
I took a blanket off the line
   The best that draped my bed
And wrapped with care his limpish form
   That soaked the tears we shed.
We are God's creatures one and all
   And each is prone to habit . . .
Fresh carrots to the hutch I took
   That once was home to rabbit . . .

Linda Zulaica

I Wonder

I wonder how many stars are in the sky
And how the seas do not run dry.
How many grains are in the sand, I wonder
How I wonder.
I wonder how no one can see the wind
That whistles through the trees
And why the sun and moon that shines upon us all
Is the same in every land throughout this world.

I wonder why - such hatred and abuse
Is hurled in every land throughout this world,
Killing, maiming is their aim
They do not care about the hurt or pain
They bring upon their fellow man
So we must do the best we can
To let them know that Jesus lived
And died to save and if they seek Him
They will find
That Jesus is a wonderful friend.

Jean Logan

INFORMATION

We hope you have enjoyed reading this book - and that you will continue to enjoy it in the coming years.

If you like reading and writing poetry drop us a line, or give us a call, and we'll send you a free information pack.

Write to :-
**Triumph House Information
Remus House
Coltsfoot Drive
Woodston
Peterborough
PE2 9JX
(01733) 898102**